# Laughter Salad

## For Little Ones

### A Gentle Mix of Nourishing Letters for Children

Kimberly Ann Borin, Ed.D.

ISBN-13: 978-1482371994
ISBN-10: 1482371995

LCCN: 2013903404

# Dedication

This book is for all of the teachers and counselors who have inspired me in and outside of the classroom. This is also for the children around the world who are always inspiring and teaching us.
We have much to learn together.

This book is also dedicated to my favorite children in the world,
Hunter and the Roses.
May you have a little bit of Valentine's Day every day.

# Acknowledgements

Thank you to all of the people in my life who offered me the blessing of an affirmation. I remember distinctly each word they said. I carry those words and phrases around like jewels. I am amazed at the power of simple words and how they continue to nourish us for a lifetime.

Thank you to all of my family, teachers, friends, and mentors. I hope this book offers a few words in return for all they have given me, and that the affirmations, letters, and moments will nourish and strengthen the adults and children who see and hear them.

# Table of Contents

# Introduction

It has always been my dream to bring together a series of letters for children. Letters are my favorite way to communicate. In this book, I wanted to create a gentle mix of letters for children . . . and for the child in all of us.

Writing this book as a series of letters was a surprise to me. I had intended to create a collection of stories and activities from my time as a counselor and teacher. However, in the midst of putting those together, it became clear that I was to *first* create a book of letters — even though I wasn't sure who the letters were for. I realized then that the stories and activities would be in the third book.

As the new idea revealed itself, I was unsure of how to create a book of letters, or where to begin. So I started listening, doodling, and writing down ideas. As I wrote, many people that I hoped might benefit from the letters flashed through my mind. I thought about children I knew that were close to me, like my nieces and nephew. I also thought about other children I knew, including family members, friends' children, and students I had known, wondering which of them might benefit from these letters.

I wondered if my letters could help families, children, counselors, and teachers who were in need of comfort, especially those who had suffered through storms and natural disasters. There were so many incidents of unspeakable horror, school shootings, and violence that also brought devastation to people's lives. It was clear that people all over the world were in need of much love, grace, and courage.

I also thought of the children I had been privileged to work with in Africa, who had stretched my definition of suffering and resilience. Their stories and their lives expanded what I understood about the strength of the human spirit and the ability to rise up, survive, and blossom against all odds. Their journeys were living proof that dreams could be brought to life with hope, positive words, supportive people, and the will to live. In the end, I wrote the letters with a wish and a prayer that they would go out into the world and be received by the people that needed them.

*Laughter Salad for Little Ones* began in bits and pieces. I started with the inspiration of a book called *Starbright Meditations for Children*, written by Maureen Garth. Her book is a collection of bedtime meditations that have helped thousands of children around the world. It is always the first book I recommend to parents whose children are worried at night. My hope was to create a book that would also bring comfort to children at bedtime — as well as in the classroom or even the counseling office.

I decided to include affirmations in my book as a way of reminding children of their importance in the world. I wanted them to know that their unique presence mattered. It was also my hope that the book would offer loving words, and wishes, just like a Valentine's Day card. Affirmations and Valentine's Day wishes are nourishing for everyone. When an affirmation is read, the person reading it benefits as well as the one hearing it. I am hoping that these affirmations bring a bit of Valentine's Day into people's everyday lives.

To make *Laughter Salad for Little Ones*, I started with the alphabet and then added affirming words and affirmations. After each affirmation, I wrote a letter to children with a few words about what the affirmation meant. Then I included some "simple moments" that can help children to feel calm, centered, and at peace.

I decided to call these activities the Seven Simple Moments. These moments involve breathing, stretching, and a chance for children to use their imaginations and relaxed minds to accept the positive words and images they create.

I hope that children will find one word, one sentence, or one simple idea that will bring more nourishment to them and their journeys. Although each letter is different, they all have the same message: "You are a gift to the world." I hope that as you read *Laughter Salad for Little Ones* you will be reminded of this so you can pursue your dreams more boldly as well.

My ultimate wish is that everyone who reads this book follows their hearts, grants themselves permission to play, and claims more freedom for their lives. As we go forward on our journeys, it is clear that the child in each of us needs this permission to have fun, rest, and to know that we are perfect as we are. We also need to know that we journey together and we are never alone.

**The Origin of _Laughter Salad_**

The title, _Laughter Salad for Little Ones,_ was modeled after my first book, _Laughter Salad, A Nourishing Mix of Inspiring Stories._ In that book, I brought together a collection of stories of synchronicity and hopefulness from my life. Those stories were inspiring to me and I hoped they would be inspiring to others. In _Laughter Salad for Little Ones,_ I hoped the letters and affirmations would have the same effect.

**Layout of the Book**

There are three main sections of _Laughter Salad for Little Ones:_
1. The Letters for Little Ones from A to Z with Illustrations
2. A Guide for the Seven Simple Moments — Ideas for Teachers, Counselors, and Parents
3. Peace Pages

**1. The Letters for Little Ones from A to Z with Illustrations**

The letters are listed from A to Z and can be read to children at bedtime, or during times of stress or uncertainty. They can also be used in schools, classrooms, and counseling offices.

The Seven Simple Moments are a series of activities that bring the letters and affirmations to life — allowing children to use breathing and their imaginations to feel calm and peaceful. When children are relaxed, they are most able to hear and absorb the affirmations and positive visualizations.

This section of the book is also good for teens and adults. The words are meant to be simple and nourishing, to bring comfort and validation. I offer them with a wish and a prayer that they provide just what you need.

**2. A Guide for _the Seven Simple Moments_ — Ideas for Teachers, Counselors, and Parents**

The Seven Simple Moments can also be the beginning of further activities in schools, classrooms, counseling offices, and at home. At the end of the book, you will find information for bringing these moments into the classroom. This chapter explores four main areas — Preparation, Process, Extension Activities, and Closure — as well as other ways to expand the Seven Simple Moments in schools.

The Seven Simple Moments include:

- Take a moment to take a deep breath in and a long breath out. If you want to take a second deep breath in and out, you can do that too!
- Take a moment to notice how you feel today, and share it if you can.
- Take a moment to notice what you need today, and share it if you can.
- Take a moment to stretch.
- Take a moment to imagine that you are a gift to the world. What does that look like to you?
- Take a moment to affirm yourself by whispering, speaking, or even singing, "I am amazing and I am a gift to the whole world."
- Take a moment to affirm others around you by whispering, speaking, or even singing, "You are a gift, and together we are a gift to the whole world."

### 3. Peace Pages

These are four simple blank pages for creating your own affirmations, lists, poems, doodles, and whatever else you'd like to write or draw. You may want to create a list of wishes, dreams for the future, things you are thankful for, or prayers.

### How to Get Started

This book can be used in many different ways. You may look up a topic or a letter of the alphabet or even turn to a random page and start there. Read in whatever order suits the needs of you, your child, your family, or your students. This book is also a beginning place for conversations that can lead to more understanding, hope, encouragement, and compassion.

### Thank You!

Thank you for taking the time to read this and share the letters, words, and inspirations with those around you. May these gentle wishes go out into the world in just the right way. My intention is to share a voice of love and encouragement for children around the globe. Thank you for reading this and for your presence; you are a gift to the whole world!

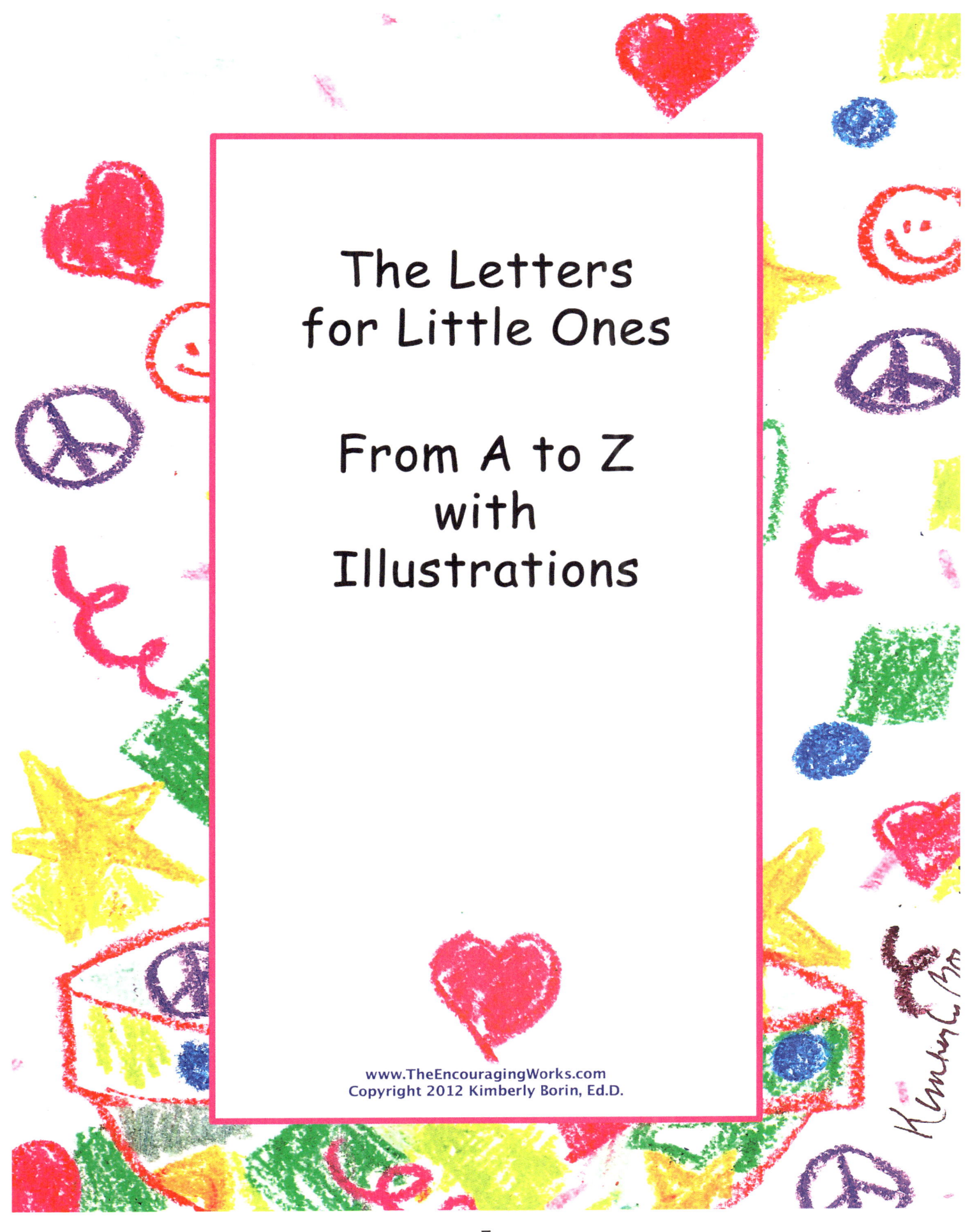

# The Letters for Little Ones

# From A to Z with Illustrations

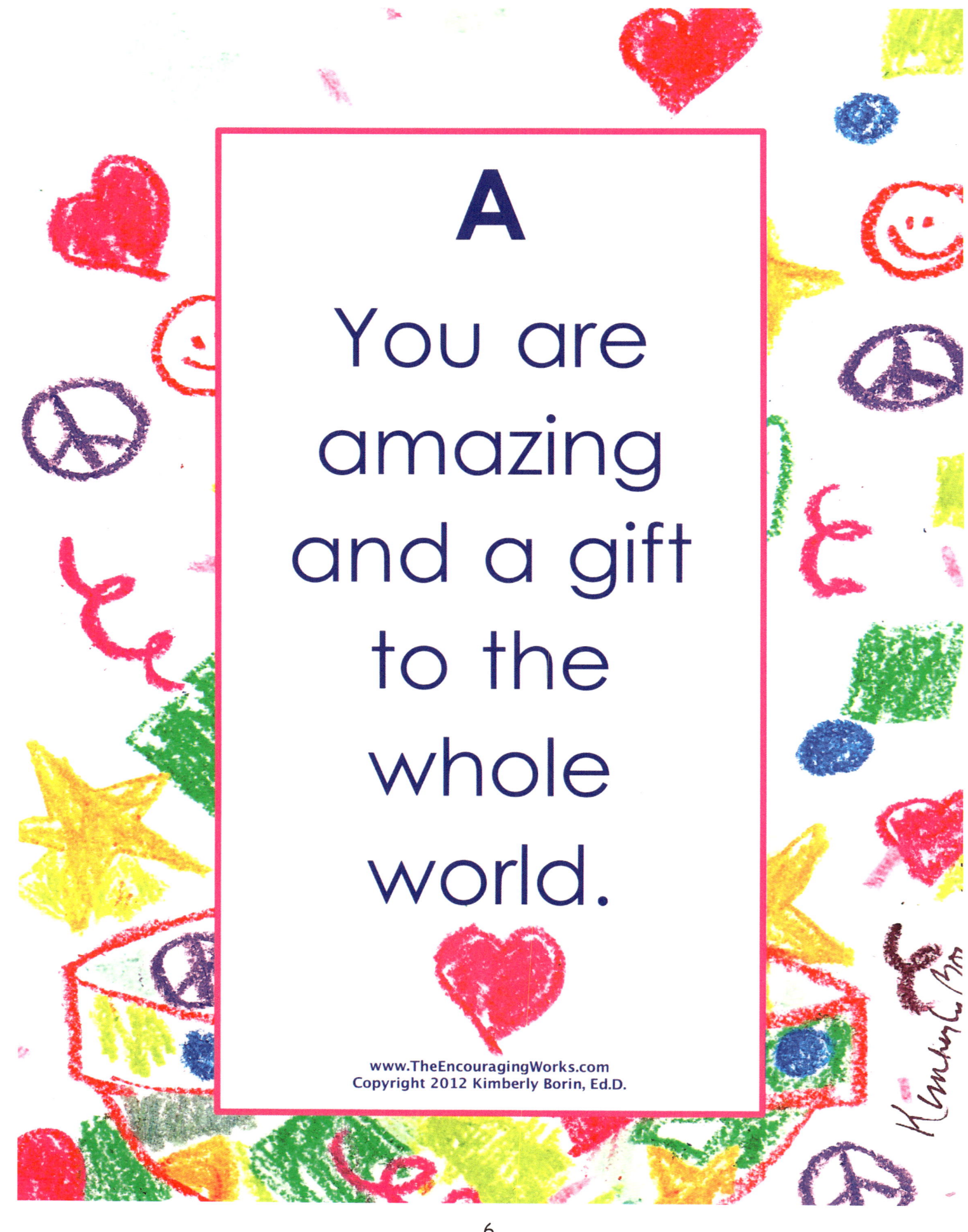

# A

You are amazing and a gift to the whole world.

# A is for Amazing

*You are amazing and a gift to the whole world!*

Dear Little One,

   This book is for you! I have written a simple note for each letter of the alphabet to remind you how special you are! For each letter, there is also an affirmation — a sentence of encouraging words — that celebrates you! I want you to know that you are amazing just as you are this very moment. The world needs you, your laugh, your smile, and your presence.

   Your unique way of being in the world also allows others to feel special and helps them on their journeys. You can bring the people around you a gift just by being yourself and just by being there. Trust that this is true!

   A is also for apple pie (yummy), answers, awake, and ant! Thank you for your amazing self!

Very sincerely,
Kimberly

**Seven Simple Moments for You…**
- Take a moment to take a deep breath in and a long breath out. If you want to take a second deep breath in and out, you can do that too!
- Take a moment to notice how you feel today, and share it if you can.
- Take a moment to notice what you need today, and share it if you can.
- Take a moment to stretch.
- Take a moment to imagine that you are a gift to the world. What does that look like to you?
- Take a moment to affirm yourself by whispering, speaking, or even singing, "I am amazing and I am a gift to the whole world."
- Take a moment to affirm others around you by whispering, speaking, or even singing, "You are a gift, and together we are a gift to the whole world."

**B**

You
are a
bright light
in the
world!
You shine!

# B is for Bright Light
## *You are a bright light in the world — you shine!*

Dear Little One,

   I want you to know that you are a bright light in the world. This means that you bring happiness and hope to others. Every time you are kind to someone, you bring a brightness, a joy to the world, one person at a time. And when people experience your kindness, they realize they can be a bright light too.

   You may sometimes feel unsure of the way things are going — or if you are noticed at all. Trust that your actions matter. Your kindness makes you a bright light to those around you — you shine!

   B is also for blessing, bear, and blossoming beautifully! Thank you for your light!

Very sincerely,
Kimberly

**Seven Simple Moments for You…**
- Take a moment to take a deep breath in and a long breath out. If you want to take a second deep breath in and out, you can do that too!
- Take a moment to notice how you feel today, and share it if you can.
- Take a moment to notice what you need today, and share it if you can.
- Take a moment to stretch.
- Take a moment to imagine that you are a bright light in the world. What does that look like to you?
- Take a moment to affirm yourself by whispering, speaking, or even singing, "I am a bright light in the world, I shine!"
- Take a moment to affirm others around you by whispering, speaking, or even singing, "You are a bright light in the world. Together, we are bright lights in the world and together, we shine!"

# C

You are cared for and our community loves you!

# C is for Cared For and Community

*You are cared for and our community loves you.*

Dear Little One,

You are very special to everyone and your community cares for you. A community is a little bit like a family — but is much larger. It's the people around you who notice you and are proud of the things you do: your friends, neighbors, people at school, and other people who will meet you too.

Because you are an important part of your community, you help to make it better. It is hard to know the impact we have on those around us, but trust that you play an important role in the family around you. Along the way, allow others to help you. We need one another and we can help each other.

C is also for courageous, creative, cat, cow, and calm. Thank you for you!

Very sincerely,
Kimberly

**Seven Simple Moments for You...**
- Take a moment to take a deep breath in and a long breath out. If you want to take a second deep breath in and out, you can do that too!
- Take a moment to notice how you feel today, and share it if you can.
- Take a moment to notice what you need today, and share it if you can.
- Take a moment to stretch.
- Take a moment to imagine that you are cared for and that your community loves you. What does that look like to you?
- Take a moment to affirm yourself by whispering, speaking, or even singing, "I am cared for and my community loves me!"
- Take a moment to affirm others around you by whispering, speaking, or even singing, "You are cared for and your community loves you. Together, we are cared for and our community loves us."

# D

You are deserving of wonderful things.

# D is for Deserving
*You are deserving of wonderful things.*

Dear Little One,

   You are deserving of so many wonderful things. This means that you deserve the best life has to offer and should expect good things for your life. Sometimes we wonder if we are "good enough" or "deserving enough" to have certain things, especially if we don't get them.

   When we don't get what we want, it's important to know that we're worthy of good things anyway. Sometimes we're in situations that aren't quite right. You may need to decide what you really want, know that you are worthy of receiving it, and take action to move toward your dreams. You have unlimited power for your life! Allow yourself to dream big and don't be afraid to ask for what you need.

   D is also for dedicated, dreams come true, dog, drum, and dancing! Thank you!

Very sincerely,
Kimberly

**Seven Simple Moments for You...**
- Take a moment to take a deep breath in and a long breath out. If you want to take a second deep breath in and out, you can do that too!
- Take a moment to notice how you feel today, and share it if you can.
- Take a moment to notice what you need today, and share it if you can.
- Take a moment to stretch.
- Take a moment to imagine that you are deserving of wonderful things. What does that look like to you?
- Take a moment to affirm yourself by whispering, speaking, or even singing, "I am deserving of wonderful things."
- Take a moment to affirm others around you by whispering, speaking, or even singing, "You are deserving of wonderful things. Together, we are deserving of wonderful things."

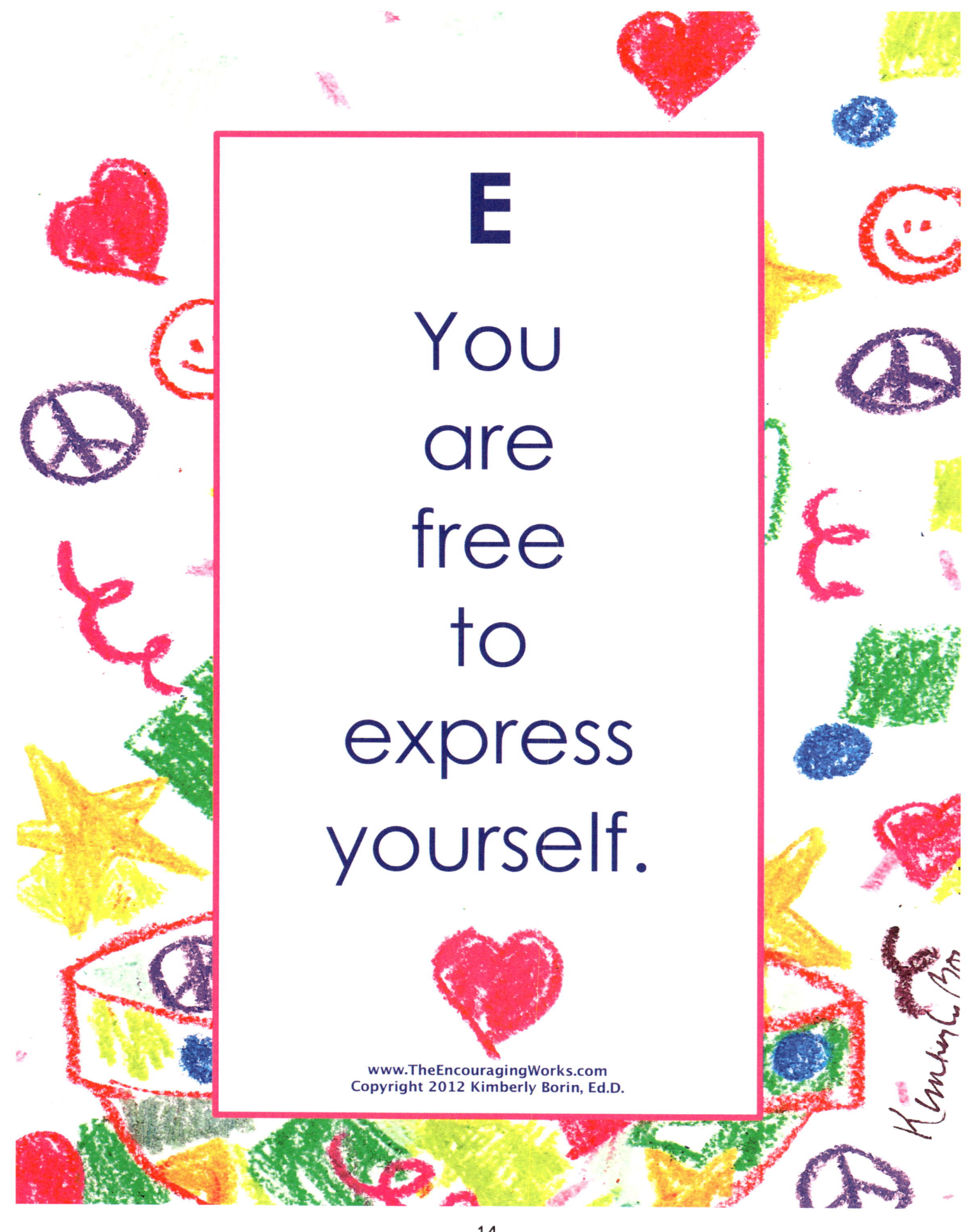

# E

## You are free to express yourself.

# E is for Express

*You are free to express yourself.*

Dear Little One,

You are free to express yourself and use your voice. This means you can give yourself permission to say what you need to say, however you need to say it. You are free to express yourself in talking, in a story, in a letter, or even in the way that you bake cookies, color, draw, or sing.

Sometimes it's hard to say what we need to say — or difficult to know how or when to say it. Trust that everything will happen at just the right time. Your timing will be perfect, and so will your words or actions. Give yourself permission to take small steps to express yourself and tell your story. It matters!

E is also for excellent, eager, elephant, and elementary! Thank you!

Very sincerely,
Kimberly

**Seven Simple Moments for You…**

- Take a moment to take a deep breath in and a long breath out. If you want to take a second deep breath in and out, you can do that too!
- Take a moment to notice how you feel today, and share it if you can.
- Take a moment to notice what you need today, and share it if you can.
- Take a moment to stretch.
- Take a moment to imagine that you are free to express yourself. What does that look like to you?
- Take a moment to affirm yourself by whispering, speaking, or even singing, "I am free to express myself."
- Take a moment to affirm others around you by whispering, speaking, or even singing, "You are free to express yourself and together we are free to express ourselves."

# F

You
are free
and
you
are
forgiven.

# F is for Free and Forgiven

*You are free and you are forgiven.*

Dear Little One,

   You are free and you are forgiven. This means that you are allowed to have freedom in your life. One way we feel free is when we are forgiven — and when we forgive others. Sometimes we may worry about whether or not we are forgiven and this can feel like a burden, making us feel stuck or ashamed.

   Trust that there is a great spirit or a God or a creative force larger than we are that forgives all of our guilt or shame. Imagine that people who have hurt you in some way are also free and forgiven. You won't have to carry around any burdens and neither will they. You are all free!

   F is also for freedom, fun, falcon, and faith. Thank you for being who you are!

Very sincerely,
Kimberly

**Seven Simple Moments for You…**
- Take a moment to take a deep breath in and a long breath out. If you want to take a second deep breath in and out, you can do that too!
- Take a moment to notice how you feel today, and share it if you can.
- Take a moment to notice what you need today, and share it if you can.
- Take a moment to stretch.
- Take a moment to imagine that you are free and are also forgiven. What does that look like to you?
- Take a moment to affirm yourself by whispering, speaking, or even singing, "I am free and I am forgiven."
- Take a moment to affirm others around you by whispering, speaking, or even singing, "You are free and you are forgiven. Together, we are free and we are forgiven."

# G

## You are a gift to the whole world. Promise!

# G is for Gift
## *You are a gift to the whole world. Promise!*

Dear Little One,

   You are a gift to the whole world. This means that you are special — and that the things you do can bring goodness to the people around you and to others far away. It's hard to imagine that you can help the whole world, but it is true. Many times when we do something small, it has a ripple effect and brings goodness to many other people. You may do something small and kind in New Jersey and it could affect someone positively in another country — or on another day.

   This is a very big idea, which takes some time to understand. As you travel on your journey, try to notice how the little things you do bring positive changes to the world. I promise that once you start to see the goodness you bring to others, you will begin to notice how even small things, like breathing, can make a difference. You are a gift! Believe it!

   G is also for goodness, giraffes, gratitude, and greatness! Thank you!

Very sincerely,
Kimberly

**Seven Simple Moments for You…**
- Take a moment to take a deep breath in and a long breath out. If you want to take a second deep breath in and out, you can do that too!
- Take a moment to notice how you feel today, and share it if you can.
- Take a moment to notice what you need today, and share it if you can.
- Take a moment to stretch.
- Take a moment to imagine that you are a gift to the whole world. What does that look like to you?
- Take a moment to affirm yourself by whispering, speaking, or even singing, "I am a gift to the whole world."
- Take a moment to affirm others around you by whispering, speaking, or even singing, "You are a gift to the whole world, and together we are a gift to the whole world."

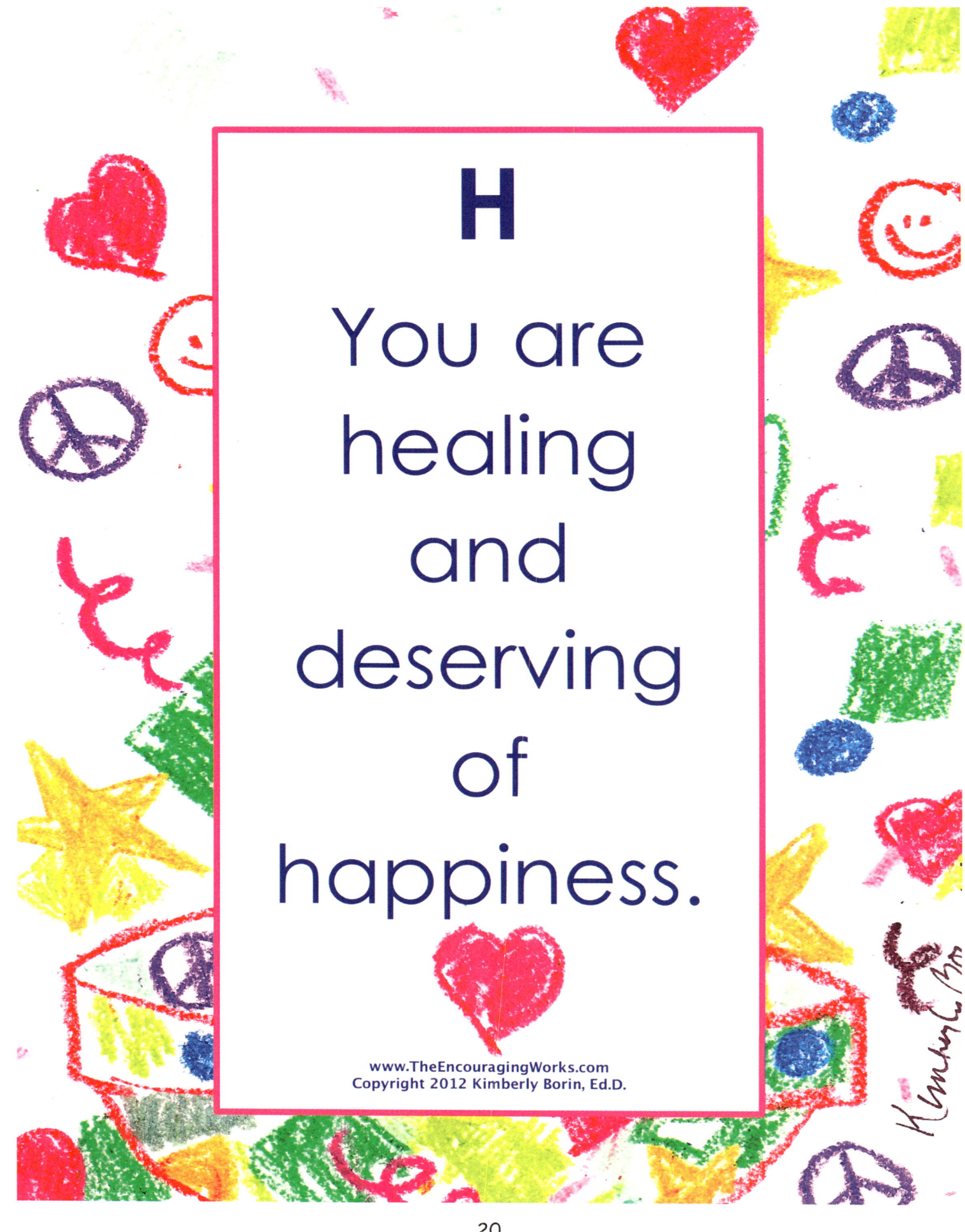

# H

You are healing and deserving of happiness.

# H is for Healing and Happiness
*You are healing and deserving of happiness.*

Dear Little One,

   You are healing and you are deserving of happiness. This means that you are getting better every day, in every way — in your mind, body, and spirit. You deserve to feel good! Sometimes our progress is small as we heal or as we are working toward feeling happier. All of the steps you are making matter and you can trust that you are becoming who you are meant to be, step by step.

   It's important to know that you deserve *every* happiness. Sometimes, there are bumps in the road and happiness doesn't seem to last or come easily. But no matter where you are, know you will heal, grow, and learn beautifully to reach greater happiness. Keep your chin up and know that you are worthy of wonderful things!

   H is also for healthy, hilarious, horse, and human being! Thank you for you!

Very sincerely,
Kimberly

**Seven Simple Moments for You...**
- Take a moment to take a deep breath in and a long breath out. If you want to take a second deep breath in and out, you can do that too!
- Take a moment to notice how you feel today, and share it if you can.
- Take a moment to notice what you need today, and share it if you can.
- Take a moment to stretch.
- Take a moment to imagine that you are healing and deserving of happiness. What does that look like to you?
- Take a moment to affirm yourself by whispering, speaking, or even singing, "I am healing and deserving of happiness."
- Take a moment to affirm others around you by whispering, speaking, or even singing, "You are healing and deserving of happiness. Together, we are healing and deserving of happiness."

I

Your imagination will help you dream and see your future.

# I is for Imagination
*Your imagination will help you dream*
*and see your future.*

Dear Little One,

   Your imagination will help you dream and see your future. It is an amazing gift that can bring your dreams to life. Your imagination will guide you to many wonderful things, especially if you visualize everything in the best, most beautiful way — with colors, sounds, smells, movement, and more.

   Use your wonderful imagination all of the time. Take the time that you need to daydream and create the picture of what you'd like for your life. Your imagination can be your road map for your dreams. I can't wait to see what good things will come true for you!

   I is also for ingenious, ice cream, instinct, igloo, insect, and international! Thank you!

Very sincerely,
Kimberly

**Seven Simple Moments for You…**
- Take a moment to take a deep breath in and a long breath out. If you want to take a second deep breath in and out, you can do that too!
- Take a moment to notice how you feel today, and share it if you can.
- Take a moment to notice what you need today, and share it if you can.
- Take a moment to stretch.
- Take a moment to notice how your imagination helps you to dream and see your future. What does that look like to you?
- Take a moment to affirm yourself by whispering, speaking, or even singing, "My imagination will help me dream and see my future."
- Take a moment to affirm others around you by whispering, speaking, or even singing, "Your imagination will help you dream and see your future. Together, our imaginations will help us dream and see our futures."

# J

You
can go
where
there
is
joy!

# J is for Joyful
## *You can go where there is joy!*

Dear Little One,

   You are allowed to go where the joy is. This means that you can move in a direction that seems nourishing —– the one that feels like it has the most joy, light, love, and happiness. Sometimes life can be very confusing, and it takes time to decide what action to take. It's important to listen to your heart and see which direction brings a smile to your face and allows you to feel at peace.

   And don't worry — you will make all of the right decisions. God is with you no matter which direction you take. I hope that wherever you go, you find joy, because when you're happy, this helps everyone around you to be happy too.

   J is also for jumping, jewel, jimmies (sprinkles), jungle, and jazzy! Thank you for you!

Very sincerely,
Kimberly

**Seven Simple Moments for You…**
- Take a moment to take a deep breath in and a long breath out. If you want to take a second deep breath in and out, you can do that too!
- Take a moment to notice how you feel today, and share it if you can.
- Take a moment to notice what you need today, and share it if you can.
- Take a moment to stretch.
- Take a moment to imagine that you can go where there is joy!  What does that look like to you?
- Take a moment to affirm yourself by whispering, speaking, or even singing, "I can go where there is joy!"
- Take a moment to affirm others around you by whispering, speaking, or even singing, "You can go where there is joy! Together we can go where there is joy!"

# K

You are kind and your kindness makes a difference!

# K is for Kind

## *You are kind and your kindness makes a difference!*

Dear Little One,

You are kind and your kindness makes a difference. This means that all of the little things you do to help others can make a very big difference, whether they are near or far away. You'll never know how much your smile, laugh, or small gift can bring happiness to others. That little bit of happiness travels out to the world and brings more love to many people.

Being kind to yourself is also important. Please take good care of yourself. This will help you to take responsibility for who you want to be. Thank you for your kindness and everything you do to make the world a better place. You make the world brighter just by showing up! We are so lucky you are here!

K is also for kangaroo, kudos, knight, and kiss! Thank you for your kindness!

Very sincerely,
Kimberly

**Seven Simple Moments for You…**
- Take a moment to take a deep breath in and a long breath out. If you want to take a second deep breath in and out, you can do that too!
- Take a moment to notice how you feel today, and share it if you can.
- Take a moment to notice what you need today, and share it if you can.
- Take a moment to stretch.
- Take a moment to imagine that you are kind and that your kindness makes a difference. What does that look like to you?
- Take a moment to affirm yourself by whispering, speaking, or even singing, "I am kind and my kindness makes a difference."
- Take a moment to affirm others around you by whispering, speaking, or even singing, "You are kind and your kindness makes a difference. Together, we are kind and our kindness makes a difference."

# L

## You are loved and you are learning beautifully too!

# L is for Loved and Learning

## *You are loved and you are learning beautifully too!*

Dear Little One,

   You are so loved and you are learning beautifully too! This means that there are many people who love and support you all of the time. This also means that along the way you are continuing to learn and grow. There is much to learn about, yet you will always learn what you need, when you need it, in your own special way. Trust that you are learning beautifully.

   Sometimes, when we are learning something new we feel frustrated or find it difficult. When that happens, don't be afraid to ask for help because many people are happy to lend a hand. Don't be afraid to ask for love also because many people are happy to let you know how special you are to them and how loved you are.

   L is also for lion, lovely, laughter, life, and light! Thank you! You are loved!

Very sincerely,
Kimberly

**Seven Simple Moments for You…**
- Take a moment to take a deep breath in and a long breath out. If you want to take a second deep breath in and out, you can do that too!
- Take a moment to notice how you feel today, and share it if you can.
- Take a moment to notice what you need today, and share it if you can.
- Take a moment to stretch.
- Take a moment to imagine that you are loved and that you are learning beautifully too! What does that look like to you?
- Take a moment to affirm yourself by whispering, speaking, or even singing, "I am loved and I am learning beautifully too!"
- Take a moment to affirm others around you by whispering, speaking, or even singing, "You are loved and you are learning beautifully! Together, we are loved and we are all learning beautifully!"

# M

You are a miracle and your presence matters!

# M is for Miracle
## *You are a miracle and your presence matters!*

Dear Little One,

   You are a miracle. There is no one like you on the planet. You are an amazing combination of cells, muscles, bones, experiences and abilities. Wherever you are, there are people who are happy you're here. There is no one like you and your special presence matters to many people.

   Sometimes we feel as though we only matter if we do something well or have something outstanding to offer. The truth is, you matter just because you are here on the planet. The world needs the gifts that you have to offer. You might also be the bearer of miracles for someone else. Believe that this is true!

   M is also for mountain, magnificent, magic, meerkat, manifestation, and music! Thank you for the miracle of you!

Very sincerely,
Kimberly

**Seven Simple Moments for You…**
- Take a moment to take a deep breath in and a long breath out. If you want to take a second deep breath in and out, you can do that too!
- Take a moment to notice how you feel today, and share it if you can.
- Take a moment to notice what you need today, and share it if you can.
- Take a moment to stretch.
- Take a moment to imagine that you are a miracle and your presence matters to everyone. What does that look like to you?
- Take a moment to affirm yourself by whispering, speaking, or even singing, "I am a miracle and my presence matters."
- Take a moment to affirm others around you by whispering, speaking, or even singing, "You are a miracle and your presence matters. Together, we are miracles and our presence matters to everyone."

# N

You are needed and important in the world.

# N is for Needed

## *You are needed and important in the world.*

Dear Little One,

   You are needed in our world and that is why you are here. This means that your presence is important to those around you because you have something special to give. You and your talents are needed to help others and to bring more love to the world.

   Sometimes, we go through a spell where we think that perhaps we aren't needed by anyone or that our contributions don't matter in the world. Trust that this is not true. Your presence is important all of the time, no matter where you are. You make a difference, and you are needed — right here, right now, right where you are. Only you can bring your special gift to the world.

   N is also for nice, nap, nature, and nautilus! Thank you for you! You are needed!

Very sincerely,
Kimberly

**Seven Simple Moments for You…**
- Take a moment to take a deep breath in and a long breath out. If you want to take a second deep breath in and out, you can do that too!
- Take a moment to notice how you feel today, and share it if you can.
- Take a moment to notice what you need today, and share it if you can.
- Take a moment to stretch.
- Take a moment to imagine that you are needed and important in the world. What does that look like to you?
- Take a moment to affirm yourself by whispering, speaking, or even singing, "I am needed and important in the world."
- Take a moment to affirm others around you by whispering, speaking or even singing, "You are needed and important in the world. Together, we are needed and important in the world."

You are
the one!
Thank you
for all that
you
are!

# O is for One

*You are the one! Thank you for all that you are!*

Dear Little One,

  You are the one! This means that only you can bring certain things to make the world a better place. You are the one who draws a certain way, writes a certain way, or rides your skateboard, surfboard, or bike in just the right way. You have a unique way of doing things in the world. It is *your* way — and this is what the world needs.

  Thank you for all that you are and all that you are becoming. Trust that as you are learning and growing, you are not alone. We are all learning together, and are so lucky that you are here! You are the one!

  O is also for octopus, outstanding, ocean, okee-dokee, and otter. Thank you for all that you are!

Very sincerely,
Kimberly

**Seven Simple Moments for You…**
- Take a moment to take a deep breath in and a long breath out. If you want to take a second deep breath in and out, you can do that too!
- Take a moment to notice how you feel today, and share it if you can.
- Take a moment to notice what you need today, and share it if you can.
- Take a moment to stretch.
- Take a moment to imagine that you are the one! What does that look like to you?
- Take a moment to affirm yourself by whispering, speaking, or even singing, "I am the one!"
- Take a moment to affirm others around you by whispering, speaking or even singing, "You are the one! Together, we are the one — and we are one!"

**P**

You are perfect as you are right now!

# P is for Perfect

## *You are perfect as you are right now!*

Dear Little One,

   You are perfect right now. This means that you are perfect just as you are in this very moment, even as you are hearing these words. Sometimes we feel we have to continually strive to be perfect, or better, or smarter, or the best. But we are all perfect just as we are right now. Trust that you are where you need to be and that you don't have to work hard to be pleasing to others.

   Take your time and grow in your own way. Only you know what you need to blossom. Take the time you need to be mindful. Listen to your heart to hear what you need to do — and then do it. Don't be afraid to ask for help along the way.

   P is also for process, playful, positive, passionate, porpoise, and polar bear! Thank you for your amazing self!

Very sincerely,
Kimberly

**Seven Simple Moments for You…**
- Take a moment to take a deep breath in and a long breath out. If you want to take a second deep breath in and out, you can do that too!
- Take a moment to notice how you feel today, and share it if you can.
- Take a moment to notice what you need today, and share it if you can.
- Take a moment to stretch.
- Take a moment to imagine that you are perfect as you are right now. What does that look like to you?
- Take a moment to affirm yourself by whispering, speaking, or even singing, "I am perfect as I am right now."
- Take a moment to affirm others around you by whispering, speaking, or even singing, "You are perfect as you are right now. Together, we are perfect as we are right now."

# Q

Your questions are important and help everyone.

# Q is for Questions
*Your questions are important and help everyone.*

Dear Little One,

Your questions are important and help everyone. This means that everything you're curious about can provide answers for others. Sometimes we feel our questions don't matter, or we may be afraid to ask them. But don't be. Oftentimes, other people have the same questions, and they're very glad someone asked.

Using your voice to ask questions takes courage. But it can bring clarity (that is a big word) to your next step and help you know you are on the right path. This will also help others find the answers they need! Your voice, your courage, and your questions and answers can inspire others to follow their dreams.

Q is also for quilt, quartz, quantum, quack, and quail. Thank you for asking!

Very sincerely,
Kimberly

**Seven Simple Moments for You...**
- Take a moment to take a deep breath in and a long breath out. If you want to take a second deep breath in and out, you can do that too!
- Take a moment to notice how you feel today, and share it if you can.
- Take a moment to notice what you need today, and share it if you can.
- Take a moment to stretch.
- Take a moment to imagine that your questions are important and help everyone. What does that look like to you?
- Take a moment to affirm yourself by whispering, speaking, or even singing, "My questions are important and help everyone."
- Take a moment to affirm others around you by whispering, speaking, or even singing, "Your questions are important and help everyone. Together, our questions are important and help everyone."

# R

## You are responsible and growing all of the time.

# R is for Responsible

## *You are responsible and growing all of the time.*

Dear Little One,

   You are responsible and growing all of the time. This means that each day, you are learning to take good care of yourself and your dreams. This is a big job. Some days, it may feel tiring or difficult to be responsible for yourself and the things you want in your life. On other days, you'll feel like celebrating — and life will seem very easy.

   Trust that you are responsible and growing every day in large ways and small ways. And know that everything you do to take care of yourself and your dreams will help others too. Be sure to ask for help when you need it. When you allow others to help you, they are affirmed in their ability to be responsible too.

   R is also for Robin Hood, reward, respect, resilience, and red wolf! Thank you!

Very sincerely,
Kimberly

**Seven Simple Moments for You…**
- Take a moment to take a deep breath in and a long breath out. If you want to take a second deep breath in and out, you can do that too!
- Take a moment to notice how you feel today, and share it if you can.
- Take a moment to notice what you need today, and share it if you can.
- Take a moment to stretch.
- Take a moment to imagine that you are responsible and growing all of the time. What does that look like to you?
- Take a moment to affirm yourself by whispering, speaking, or even singing, "I am responsible and growing all of the time."
- Take a moment to affirm others around you by whispering, speaking, or even singing, "You are responsible and growing all of the time. Together, we are responsible and growing all of the time."

# S

# You are safe and can be silly if you want to.

# S is for Safe and Silly

*You are safe and you can be silly if you want to.*

Dear Little One,

   You are safe — and you can be silly if you want to. This means you deserve to always feel safe, and you also have the right to be silly. Sometimes when we want to be silly, we feel nervous or worried about what others might think. If we don't feel safe, we don't want to be playful. But you deserve to feel safe all of the time and are allowed to have fun, laugh, be yourself, and play.

   When you don't feel safe, it is very important to tell someone because there are many people who love you and want you to feel safe. When people who love you surround you, you can be more of yourself and blossom into the person you've always wanted to be. You deserve to feel safe and happy.

   S is also for stupendous, swing, sweet, sunshine, snowflake, and sea otter. Thank you for all that you are and all that you are becoming!

Very sincerely,
Kimberly

**Seven Simple Moments for You…**
- Take a moment to take a deep breath in and a long breath out. If you want to take a second deep breath in and out, you can do that too!
- Take a moment to notice how you feel today, and share it if you can.
- Take a moment to notice what you need today, and share it if you can.
- Take a moment to stretch.
- Take a moment to imagine that you are safe and that you can be silly if you want to. What does that look like to you?
- Take a moment to affirm yourself by whispering, speaking, or even singing, "I am safe, and I can be silly if I want to."
- Take a moment to affirm others around you by whispering, speaking, or even singing, "You are safe and you can be silly if you want to. Together, we are safe and we can be silly if we want to."

# T

You are tremendous and trusted by others. Thank You!

# T is for Tremendous, Trusted, and Thank You!

*You are tremendous and trusted by others. Thank you!*

Dear Little One,

You are tremendous and because of who you are, others trust you. This means that people can count on you. Your character and trustworthiness make a difference to those around you. Sometimes we worry about not doing the right thing, or making a mistake. Trust that you are a tremendous person of character and that you have something to offer others, even when you make a mistake.

When you are trustworthy and strong for yourself, you help others move forward in their lives and in their dreams. You will attract people who believe in you and want to be with you. In this way, you create a strong and loving community — which can change the world!

T is also for tiger, transformation, treasure, truck, tune, and trout! Thank you!

Very sincerely,
Kimberly

**Seven Simple Moments for You…**
- Take a moment to notice how you feel today.
- Take a moment to notice what you need today.
- Take a moment to stretch.
- Take a moment to take a deep breath in and a long breath out.
- Take a moment to imagine that you are tremendous and trusted by others. What does that look like to you?
- Take a moment to affirm yourself by whispering, speaking, or even singing, "I am tremendous and trusted by others."
- Take a moment to affirm others around you by whispering, speaking, or even singing, "You are tremendous and trusted by others. Together, we are tremendous and trusted by others."

# U

## You are capable of understanding many things.

# U is for Understanding
## *You are capable of understanding many things.*

Dear Little One,

You are capable of understanding many things. This means that you have an amazing ability to learn new things in many areas of life. At times, you may be confused, but trust that you will understand what you need and the answers will come. You have the ability to be still, to listen to your heart, and to learn. Some things take a little longer to understand, but they will eventually become clear to you.

You are also smart and have a strong intuition. Trust your "gut feelings" and take all the time you need to decide what to do in situations that feel confusing. It's also important to reach out to others if you don't understand something or are confused. There are many people around you who want to help.

U is also for ukulele, ultramarathon, undaunted (wow - that is a very big word), unique, and umbrella bird. Thank you!

Very sincerely,
Kimberly

**Seven Simple Moments for You…**
- Take a moment to take a deep breath in and a long breath out. If you want to take a second deep breath in and out, you can do that too!
- Take a moment to notice how you feel today, and share it if you can.
- Take a moment to notice what you need today, and share it if you can.
- Take a moment to stretch.
- Take a moment to imagine that you are capable of understanding many things. What does that look like to you?
- Take a moment to affirm yourself by whispering, speaking, or even singing, "I am capable of understanding many things!"
- Take a moment to affirm others around you by whispering, speaking, or even singing, "You are capable of understanding many things. Together, we are capable of understanding many things."

# V

Your voice,
your story,
and
your
vision
matter.

# V is for Voice and Vision

*Your voice, your story, and your vision matter.*

Dear Little One,

   Your voice, your story, and your vision matter. This means you have a unique imagination that gives you creative ideas and inspiration. You also have a special way of expressing those ideas, whether it's in drawings, or in the way you bake, or even how you ride a skateboard. We call this expression of yourself your "voice." The more you use your voice, the more you breathe life into the person you have wanted to be.

   Give yourself quiet time and space to daydream and imagine what you would like in your life. Then share these stories about your life, as they might inspire other people to reach their goals and dreams. Take small, simple steps to begin to breathe life into your vision.

   We can't wait to see what amazing things you will to bring to the world! Thank you in advance! V is also for Valentine's Day, victories, vitality, and vulture (yikes!).

Very sincerely,
Kimberly

**Seven Simple Moments for You…**
- Take a moment to take a deep breath in and a long breath out. If you want to take a second deep breath in and out, you can do that too!
- Take a moment to notice how you feel today, and share it if you can.
- Take a moment to notice what you need today, and share it if you can.
- Take a moment to stretch.
- Take a moment to imagine that your voice, your story, and your vision matter. What does that look like to you?
- Take a moment to affirm yourself by whispering, speaking, or even singing, "My voice, my story, and my vision matter!"
- Take a moment to affirm others around you by whispering, speaking, or even singing, "Your voice, your story, and your vision matter. Together, our voices, our stories, and our visions matter to the whole world."

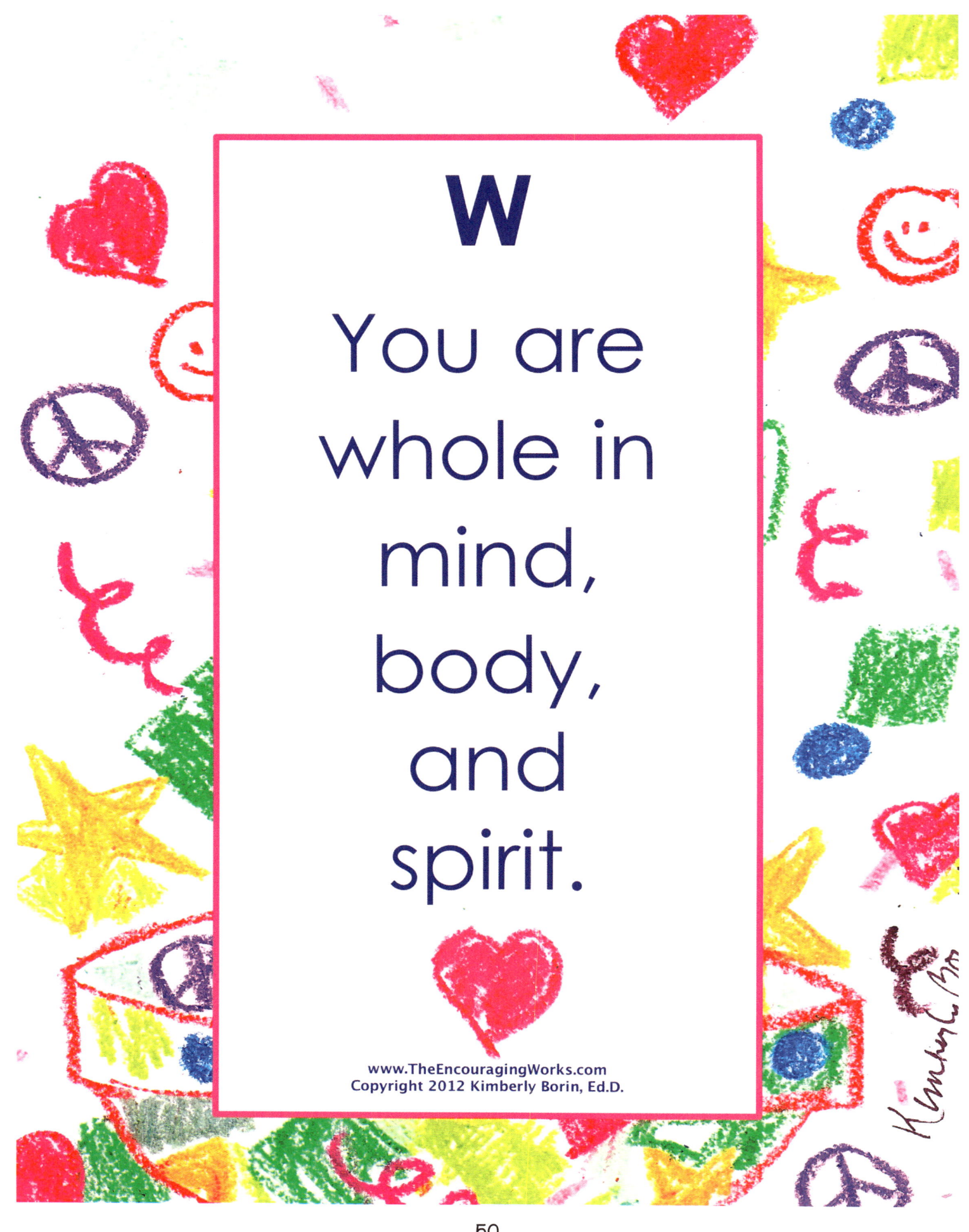

# W

You are whole in mind, body, and spirit.

# W is for Whole

*You are whole in mind, body, and spirit.*

Dear Little One,

 You are whole in mind, body, and spirit. This means that you are perfect just as you are. Sometimes we feel we are not good enough or smart enough or strong enough or whole enough. We feel this way because we are human and we compare ourselves to others; this is a very normal feeling.

 But it's important to know that even if we don't feel perfect sometimes, we are perfect at every moment. And we're constantly becoming more and more complete, more whole, and more of who we are meant to be. This helps us to bring more love to the world — a very big and important job. We are all in this together, and we are all growing to be the best person we can be.  You are not alone!

 W is also for wonder, wonderful, wishes, wings, water, world, whale, and most importantly, WE! Thank you!

Very sincerely,
Kimberly

**Seven Simple Moments for You…**
- Take a moment to take a deep breath in and a long breath out. If you want to take a second deep breath in and out, you can do that too!
- Take a moment to notice how you feel today, and share it if you can.
- Take a moment to notice what you need today, and share it if you can.
- Take a moment to stretch.
- Take a moment to imagine that you are whole in mind, body, and spirit. What does that look like to you?
- Take a moment to affirm yourself by whispering, speaking, or even singing, "I am whole in mind, body, and spirit."
- Take a moment to affirm others around you by whispering, speaking, or even singing, "You are whole in mind, body, and spirit. Together, we are whole in mind, body, and spirit."

# X

# You are exceptional in every way.

# X is for Exceptional
*You are exceptional in every way.*

Dear Little One,

   You are exceptional in every way. This means that you have unique qualities, special gifts and talents, and a special smile. You play a very important role in the world and bring goodness to the lives of others. You can share your light just by being yourself.

   Sometimes it takes courage to be who you are. It takes confidence and fearlessness to stand fully in your presence on the planet. But trust that all the courage, strength, and faith you desire will show up whenever you need it. Know that you're exceptional just as you are right now, and take time to celebrate your amazing self!

   X is also for xylophone, x-ray, Xanadu, and Xhosa! Thank you!

Very sincerely,
Kimberly

**Seven Simple Moments for You...**
- Take a moment to take a deep breath in and a long breath out. If you want to take a second deep breath in and out, you can do that too!
- Take a moment to notice how you feel today, and share it if you can.
- Take a moment to notice what you need today, and share it if you can.
- Take a moment to stretch.
- Take a moment to imagine that you are exceptional in every way. What does that look like to you?
- Take a moment to affirm yourself by whispering, speaking, or even singing, "I am exceptional in every way!"
- Take a moment to affirm others around you by whispering, speaking, or even singing, "You are exceptional in every way. Together, we are exceptional in every way."

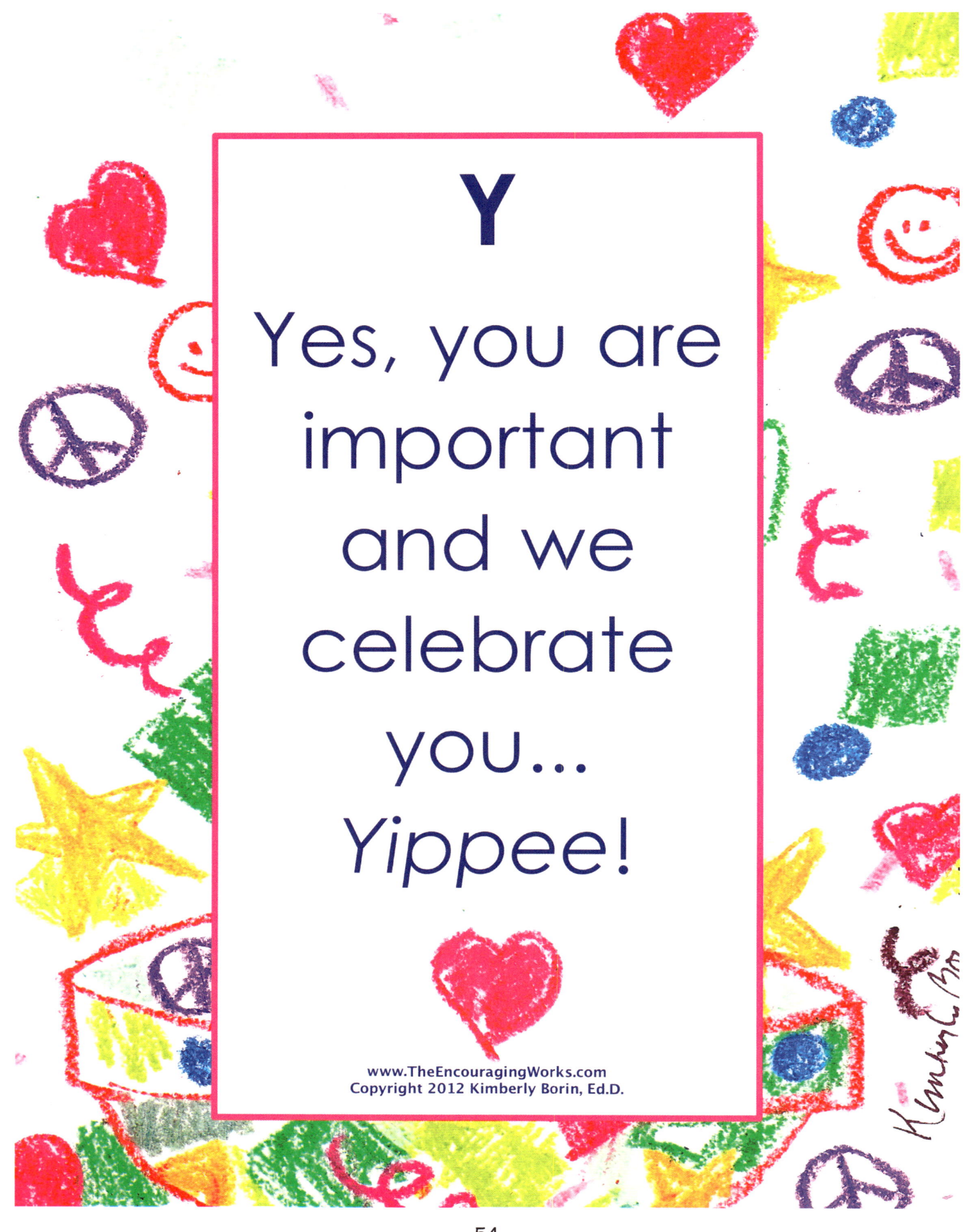

# Y

Yes, you are important and we celebrate you... *Yippee!*

# Y is for Yes and Yippee!

*Yes, you are important and we celebrate you . . . Yippee!*

Dear Little One,

Yes, you are important and we celebrate who you are becoming. This means that within you is a dream for your life that you can listen for and follow. This dream will reveal itself to you in small ways through ideas, inspirations, and perhaps even a whisper or two. This gentle nudging will help you know what direction to go, what actions to take, and where to find nourishment for your mind, body, and spirit.

In time, others will see how you're following your heart, which will inspire them to also follow their hearts. Thank you for your courage in listening to your dreams and bringing them to life.

Y is also for you, yak, youth, yoga, and yesterday! Thank you and Yippee for You!

Very sincerely,
Kimberly

**Seven Simple Moments for You...**
- Take a moment to take a deep breath in and a long breath out. If you want to take a second deep breath in and out, you can do that too!
- Take a moment to notice how you feel today, and share it if you can.
- Take a moment to notice what you need today, and share it if you can.
- Take a moment to stretch.
- Take a moment to imagine that you are important and you are celebrated. What does that look like to you?
- Take a moment to affirm yourself by whispering, speaking, or even singing, "Yes, I am important and I am celebrated!"
- Take a moment to affirm others around you by whispering, speaking, or even singing, "Yes, you are important and we celebrate you . . . Together, we are important and we are celebrated. Yippee!"

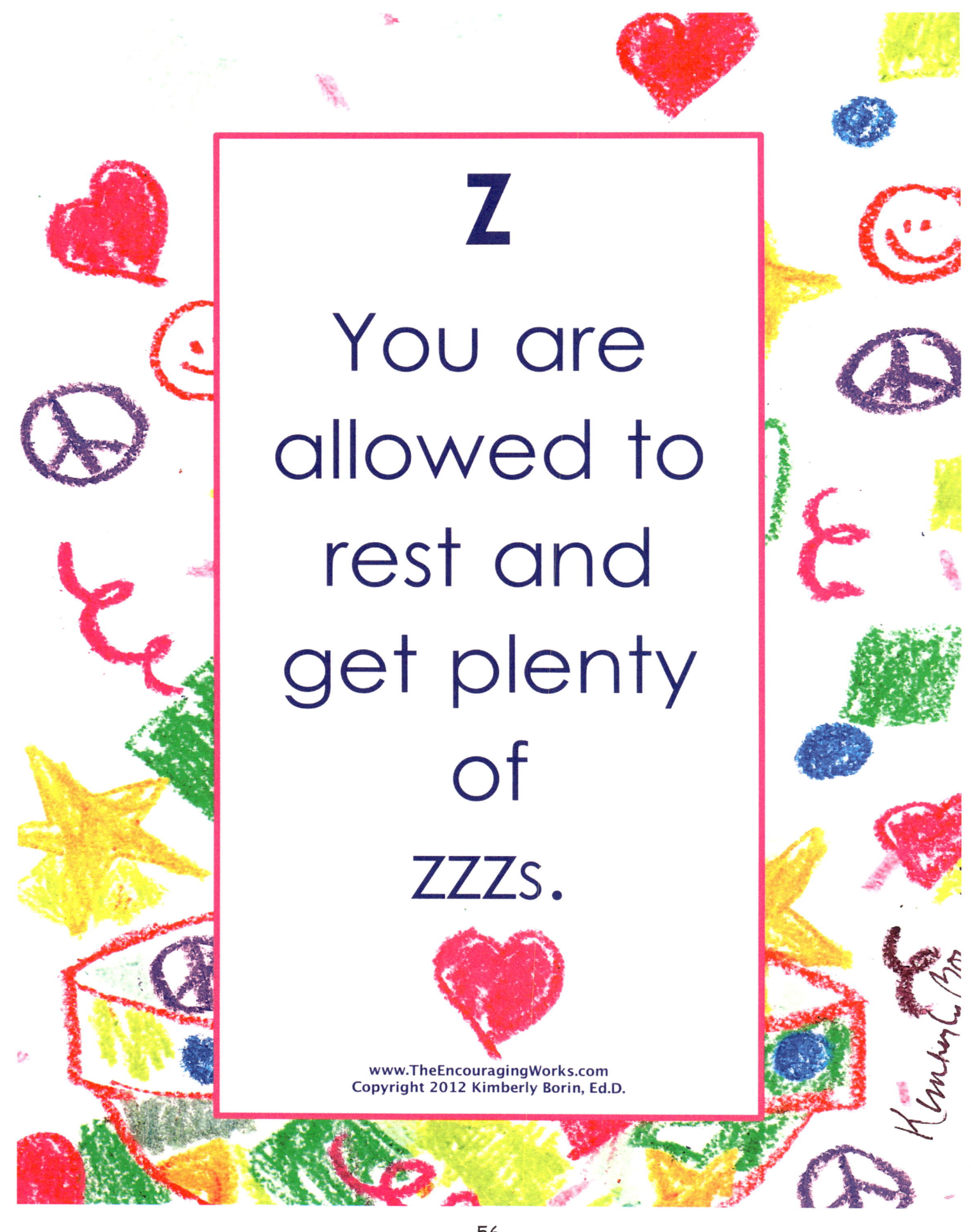

# Z

You are allowed to rest and get plenty of ZZZs.

# Z is for ZZZs
## *You are allowed to rest and get plenty of zzzs.*

Dear Little One,

You are allowed to rest and get plenty of zzzs. This means that you can take a break when you need to! When you offer yourself sleep, and maybe even a nap, you allow your brain to rest and your body to heal and be re-energized. It is so important to take good care of yourself all of the time. When you feel healthy and rested, you will be able to bring your dreams to life and be happy.

We sometimes think we have to work hard all the time. But it's better to have a balance of work, play, and rest. So give yourself permission to rest and play — in addition to work — which will also help others give themselves permission to rest and play. This will allow everyone to feel happier.

Z is also for zebra, zoo, Zen, and zing! Thank you for your presence and for reading the book too!

Very sincerely,
Kimberly


**Seven Simple Moments for You…**
- Take a moment to take a deep breath in and a long breath out. If you want to take a second deep breath in and out, you can do that too!
- Take a moment to notice how you feel today, and share it if you can.
- Take a moment to notice what you need today, and share it if you can.
- Take a moment to stretch.
- Take a moment to imagine that you are allowed to rest and get plenty of zzzs. What does that look like to you?
- Take a moment to affirm yourself by whispering, speaking, or even singing, "I am allowed to rest and get plenty of zzzs."
- Take a moment to affirm others around you by whispering, speaking, or even singing, "You are allowed to rest and get plenty of zzzzs. We are allowed to rest and get plenty of zzzzs."

# Peace Pages

The Peace Pages are blank pages for you to use in the way you see fit. You can use them to create your own affirmations, drawings, wishes, or prayers too.
Have fun and you may want to share your positive words and expressions with others!

www.TheEncouragingWorks.com
Copyright 2012 Kimberly Borin, Ed.D.

www.TheEncouragingWorks.com
Copyright 2012 Kimberly Borin, Ed.D.

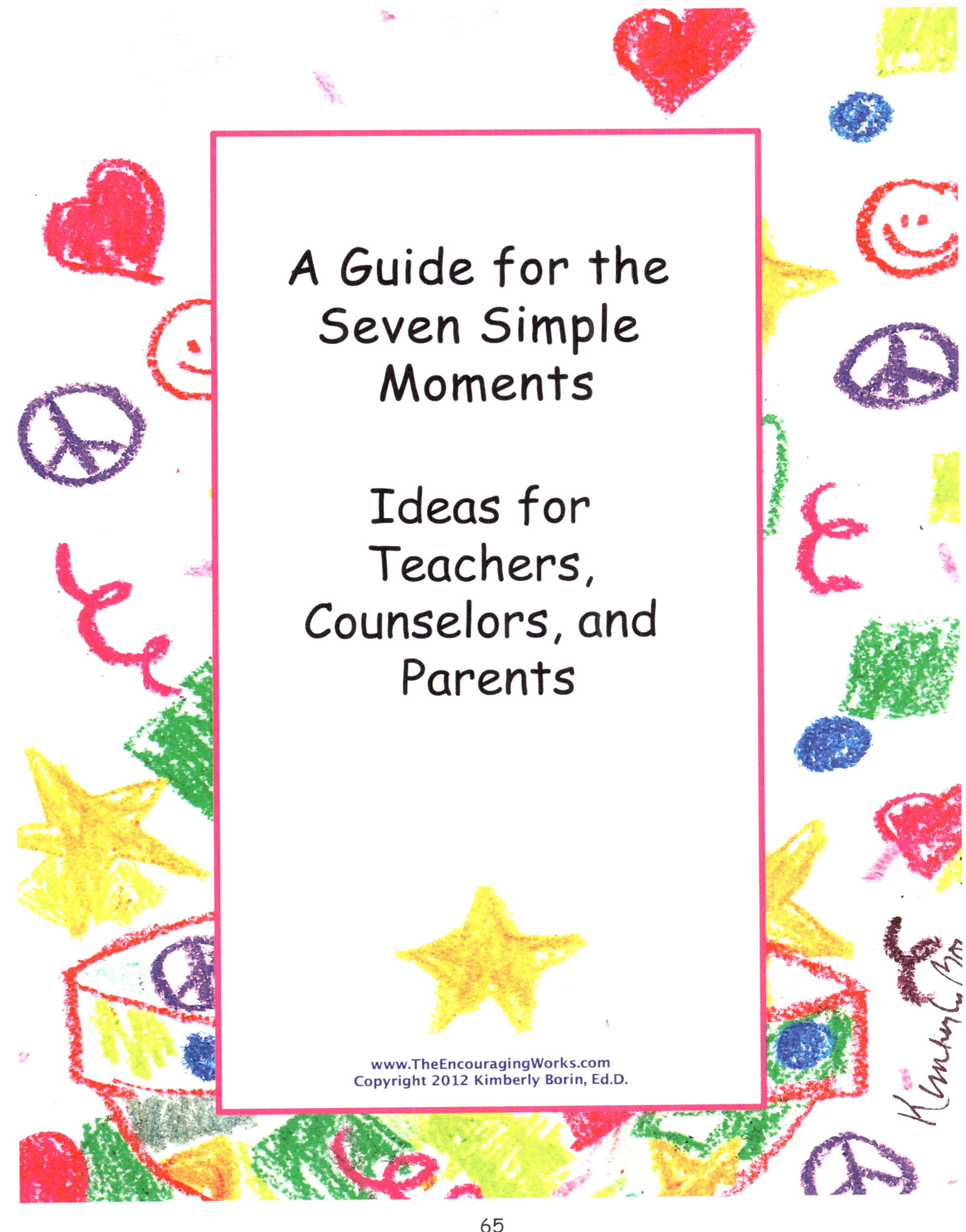

# A Guide for the Seven Simple Moments

# Ideas for Teachers, Counselors, and Parents

# A Guide for the Seven Simple Moments — Ideas for Teachers, Counselors, and Parents

The Seven Simple Moments are the exercises at the end of each letter. They are meant to be easy for parents and children, especially when children are doing them before going to sleep. Educators may also want to bring these activities into the classroom, the counseling office, or even to recess.

These seven nourishing moments bring positive energy, peace, and strength to our minds, bodies, and spirits. They can be done one small moment at a time, or all seven together. Sometimes the moments can lead to simple conversations when children and adults express how they are feeling. This can create greater understanding and compassion for one another.

**The Seven Simple Moments include:**
- Take a moment to take a deep breath in and a long breath out. If you want to take a second deep breath in and out, you can do that too!
- Take a moment to notice how you feel today, and share it if you can.
- Take a moment to notice what you need today, and share it if you can.
- Take a moment to stretch.
- Take a moment to imagine that you are a gift to the world. What does that look like to you?
- Take a moment to affirm yourself by whispering, speaking, or even singing, "I am a gift to the world!"
- Take a moment to affirm others around you by whispering, speaking, or even singing, "You are a gift to the world and together we are a gift to the world!"

**Benefits of the Seven Simple Moments**

These activities can strengthen:
- awareness of mind, body, spirit, and mindfulness
- self-care
- breathing
- visualization
- positive self-talk
- stories and expression

- compassion for others and understanding our global connection
- relaxation and resilience
- self-soothing, inner peace, and sense of calm
- learning, concentration, and focus
- goal setting and moving toward our dreams
- creating a peaceful family, school and community
- flexibility in mind, body, and spirit

## How to Use the 'Moments' in the Classroom or Counseling Office

Below are the four key elements of teaching the Seven Simple Moments in the classroom: Preparation, Process, Extension Activities, and Closure.

## PREPARATION

**Ideas for the Facilitator** — In being a facilitator of activities meant for relaxation, it is important to notice your tone of voice, your personal energy, and the energy of the group. It is imperative to use a very gentle, natural, and slow tone of voice. It is also important to be aware of how you feel. If you are having a difficult day, it may be harder to feel calm. You may also want to notice how the children are feeling and adapt the activities to their energy.

**Choosing the Exercises** — In choosing the exercises, you may want to start in a very simple way. Select one thing that seems appealing and start there. When you feel comfortable about adding something else, do that next. Work in the way that is most nourishing to you as the facilitator. The peace and comfort you feel will help the children the most.

**Sharing with Parents** — It is important to share with parents what you are doing in the classroom or counseling office. If you teach parents what you are doing, they might want to try it too. Some parents aren't comfortable with breathing exercises for a variety of reasons, so it's best to ask for their permission.

## PROCESS

**Proper Introduction and Closure** — When you begin each exercise, be sure to explain its purpose. Also, describe in detail what you will be doing. When students are doing something new, like breathing, saying affirmations, or even stretching, they need to know what to expect. They don't want to feel embarrassed or silly, so letting them know your plan helps them feel safe in trying something new.

**Safety** — Teaching about affirmations, breathing, and relaxation in the classroom can require more tenderness, love, and care than usual. Traditionally, we don't speak about these kinds of things in classrooms, and when we do, children need to feel safe enough to reveal their hopes, dreams, and feelings. Talk about the need for safety in the classroom and why it matters. It's important to check in frequently with everyone to make sure they feel OK.

**Rules** — Decide as a teacher or a class on the rules so that everyone can relax. Explain that the rules will protect your students from feeling vulnerable because it's important to honor their experiences. It is important to set up some simple rules about talking, respecting the experiences of others, and confidentiality.

**Explaining the Concepts** — Some of the ideas in the letters are very big concepts for young minds. These ideas may require some explanation and further examples for clarification. Some students will understand these concepts easily, even if they are young, while others may need more discussion.

**Approach** — The process of the activities is up to you! You may want to go through them alphabetically, methodically, or even randomly. With the Seven Simple Moments, you can choose one moment, all of them, or none. The children may also have their own ideas on how to bring the affirmations to life.

**Student Needs** — As a teacher or counselor, you are very aware of all your students' needs. Try to plan for these ahead of time to help students with attention, processing, or sensory issues. Be sure to explain everything thoroughly and make adaptations when necessary.

**Stress** — It can be helpful to talk about stress — where it comes from, how it manifests itself, how we cope with it, and how often it might occur. When students understand why they're stressed, it helps them understand when and why they need to breathe, move, visualize, or use affirmations. It can be helpful to incorporate a bit of science so that students might understand the parts of the brain that when relaxed (the amygdala) help them to learn (the prefrontal cortex), remember (the hippocampus) and make good choices (the prefrontal cortex).

**Laughter** — It's good to tell children that when learning about relaxation, affirmations, or even breathing, they may feel silly. It's important for them to know that we can all laugh together during the beginning of the exercises. It's also good to set limits on the laughter so that when people want to be serious they won't be interrupted by laughter or feel they are being laughed at.

**Religion** — Ask if anyone is not comfortable with the activities for religious reasons or otherwise. Allow students the option of not participating for the entire lesson or even a small part. If they are unsure, they may want to check with their parents or you may want to check with their parents.

**Eyes** — Offer students the option of closing their eyes or not.
Some students will want to close their eyes during relaxation exercises while others will not want to, or may even feel afraid.

**Feet** — Be sure that your students' feet are on the floor. This will help them feel safe and grounded, which is very important for doing breath work.

**Courage** — Affirm their courage and bravery in trying relaxation skills. These skills are not easy, and some students may feel embarrassed and need a lot of encouragement. It is courageous to try something new, especially things like breathing, imagining or stretching in a group setting.


## EXTENSION ACTIVITIES

Below, I offer some extensions and alternatives for the Seven Simple Moments. Please consider these various lists a starting point, as I imagine that you and your students will come up with many other ideas to try.

### Focusing on the Words

Within the 26 affirmations are life-giving words. You may want to use these words in other ways, or even add more words for each letter of the alphabet.

1. Amazing
2. Bright Light
3. Cared For and Community
4. Deserving
5. Express
6. Free and Forgiven
7. Gift
8. Healing and Happiness
9. Imagination
10. Joyful
11. Kind
12. Loved and Learning
13. Miracle
14. Needed
15. One
16. Perfect
17. Questions
18. Responsible
19. Safe and Silly
20. Tremendous, Trusted, and Thank You
21. Understanding
22. Voice and Vision
23. Whole
24. Exceptional
25. Yes and Yippee!
26. ZZZs

**Ideas for Greater Awareness**

The Seven Simple Moments are meant to help children become aware of how they are feeling and offer them a chance to breathe and find their own center. When children become aware of how they're feeling or what they need, they can begin to move in a direction that will be the most nourishing, helpful, or healing. The greater their awareness as they grow, the more they will be able to take care of themselves and be empowered to follow their dreams. Below are some other suggestions for awareness.

Help children to notice:

- their feelings in the moment — or about the day.
- how they would like to feel.
- their thoughts in the moment.
- their energy in the moment.
- how their bodies feel.
- their breathing.
- what they need for the moment.
- anything else that's happening with them.

## Movement Ideas

It is important for children (and all of us) to move, even if in simple ways. Below is a list of movement techniques. It is a good idea to do these movements with an awareness of the breath, which will also bring more awareness to the body and mind. With children, it is easy to be creative with movement, breathing, and laughter!

- moving arms, hands, fingers
- moving the head and face
- moving legs and knees
- moving shoulders and back
- moving the feet
- moving side to side
- moving forward and backwards
- moving quickly and then slowly
- moving with breath
- using progressive relaxation (tensing and releasing the muscles in the body)
- using yoga moves
- using movements that "cross the midline" (these are simple movements where arms and legs cross the center line of the body)
- wiggling fingers and toes
- moving to music
- laughing
- dancing
- turning

- walking
- standing
- jumping

## Inspiring Things to Imagine

Children often have very vivid imaginations. It is easy for them to visualize scenes in their minds, especially when they are given the time, space and permission to do so. Each of the moments has its own visualization that goes with each affirmation, but I have included some additional ideas to imagine below.

- **Nature** — animals, trees, insects, butterflies, waterfalls, bears, flowers, fireflies, dragonflies, horses, dogs, breezes, the sun, seashells, stars, gardens, fruit, vegetables, dolphins, whales, frogs, rainbows, or anything in nature that is inspiring!
- **Landscapes** — the ocean, the forest, the beach, the mountains, the African plains, a river, the desert, the rain forest, a meadow of flowers, a city, etc.
- **Time** — the future, the past, right now.
- **Elements of Comfort** — blankets, hot chocolate, ice cream, people who love them, their favorite place to be, their favorite thing to wear, their favorite food, special celebrations, birthday parties, cupcakes, etc.
- **Moving Items** — trains, cars, skateboards, trucks, surfboards, sailboats, magic carpets, bicycles, etc.
- **Magical Things** — rainbows, wishes, fairies, angels, sparkles, gems, hidden treasures, light(s), unicorns, parties, presents, dreams come true, etc.
- **People** — family, friends, people who love you, heroes, people you'd like to meet, and cartoon characters too.
- **Pathways** — a garden path, a nature trail, a road, a river, a magical sidewalk, a path of gems, a sparkling road, etc.
- **Elements of Play** — playground, amusement park, toys, slides, pinwheels, beach balls, jump ropes, crayons, the park, a vacation spot, etc.
- **Senses** — sounds, smells, colors, textures, tastes, feelings, music, etc.
- **Verbs** — walking, dancing, singing, jumping, playing, sleeping, creating, drawing, swimming, healing, growing, being successful, learning, etc.

**Extending the Affirmations in Creative Ways**

The affirmations are presented in a simple way and children are encouraged to say them. There are so many things that you can do with the affirmations and positive words. The more children engage, create, and express positive thoughts and beliefs about themselves, the more they will learn to breathe life into their dreams and develop resilience on the journey. Below is a simple list of other ways to create and celebrate life-giving words.

- write a letter
- draw
- paint
- sculpt
- talk
- act
- sing
- dance
- create a party
- move
- color
- make a collage
- bake a cake
- take a photo
- write a blog
- make a weaving
- glue something together
- dress up
- create a bouquet
- plant something
- sew
- make an ice cream sundae
- build something
- create music
- help someone
- go for a walk
- play a game
- look for treasure
- create a card
- design on the computer

- write a poem
- daydream


**Other Ways to Keep Relaxation Playful**

In addition to creating the affirmations in new ways, you can also bring in elements of play. Affirmations and play can also be relaxing. When working with young children (and sometimes older children too), there are materials you can bring that encourage more playful relaxation.

**Art**
- Have students draw an image of their visualization.
- Have students choose colors that show how they'd like to feel and how they currently feel.
- Have students draw to peaceful and relaxing music.
- Have students use their breath while drawing, inhaling as they move the crayon one way and exhaling as they move the crayon another way.
- Use collages, clay, paint, sand, or any other material to allow students to express how they feel and how they'd like to feel.
- Look at art or photos that bring a sense of peace and explore why.

**Nature and Animals**
- Talk with students about the animals they love — pets or otherwise.
- Ask what those animals teach them
- Ask which animals inspire them, and why.
- Take a walk outside and allow students to see what they learn from nature about stillness, strength, and blossoming.
- Ask them about their favorite moment in nature. Their answers are often something awe-inspiring and peaceful.

**Books, Music and Toys**
- Look for books that celebrate peace.
- Have an older student write a message affirming the peace that a young person brings to the world.
- Have students listen to all kinds of music, and bring in some of their own.
- Use simple toys like pinwheels, Play-Doh™, bubbles, bouncing balls, etc.

## CLOSURE

It is important to close the class with a special ritual or a gentle ending so that students can return to their schoolwork. This means not ending the exercises abruptly — but allowing some transition time between coming out of relaxation and preparing to enter into the process of work — or leaving the classroom and going into a noisy hallway.

**Feedback** — You may want to ask for feedback to see if students will share anything about their experiences. Because they may still feel vulnerable, you may only find one or two students who are willing to share.

**Practice** — We want students to know that practicing breathing, simple movements, and affirmations is very important. We also want them to understand that this is a life-long process. Let students know that when they practice these simple strategies, their ability to relax becomes more automatic — especially as they get older.

**Giving Thanks and Making a Wish** — I always offer students a thank you at the end of the exercises. It is important for children to know that all the little things they are doing to take care of themselves can make a positive difference in the world. I often end relaxation lessons with students (and my adult yoga classes) by having them send a positive wish out into the world and one for themselves. They can choose a person, a situation, a country, an animal, even the Tooth Fairy! They always seem to enjoy this and feel happy about sending good thoughts out to others.

# About the Author

Dr. Kimberly Borin has been working in education since 1989 and has served as an elementary school teacher as well as an elementary and high school counselor. She earned her doctorate in 2005 from Rutgers University in social and philosophical foundations of education. She earned a master of education degree in college counseling and student personnel administration from the University of Delaware in 1989 and a master of arts degree in educational leadership in 2010 from Centenary College.

She has worked with students in South Africa, Egypt, and as a Fulbright Group Scholar in Swaziland. For her doctoral research, Kimberly gathered children's stories about their favorite moments in nature. She loves to design programs that help children explore and experience mindfulness, relaxation, and resilience in playful and peaceful ways.

She has also taught *Storywriting* to children and adults since 1991 and has been working with children in schools and private settings since 1987. Whenever she works with children and adults, she can't help but want to share stories and listen to the stories of others. Hearing their stories is life-giving and affirming to both the teller and listener.

Kimberly is also a yoga teacher, certified in the Ananda yoga tradition. She has received level one certification and is registered as an R.Y.T. (Registered Yoga Teacher) at the 200-hour level. She is also trained as a Karma Kids Yoga Instructor through Karma Kids Yoga in New York City. She is also a certified Laugh Yoga Leader and is trained in Restorative and Therapeutic Yoga. Kimberly loves teaching yoga to children and adults because it helps everyone on all levels. She teaches at schools, retreat centers, and through her business, Encouraging Works! You can find more information on her website and blogs at: www.theencouragingworks.com

Whenever she has time (or a snow day from school), she loves to create art. Her work focuses on words that encourage, uplift, and heal. She creates prints, collages, cards, and yoga mats too! Her artwork can be found at: http://kimberlyannborin.zenfolio.com

Kimberly also completed a yearlong program in Contemplative Prayer and has been a reiki healer since 2000. She teaches all three levels of reiki healing. She sees reiki as a healing energy and a form of healing and contemplative prayer.

She hopes you might check out her first book of memoirs, *Laughter Salad, A Nourishing Mix of Inspiring Stories,* and her next book: *Learning and Growing with Laughter Salad.* One of the stories from her first book was also published in *GodWink Stories, A Devotional,* written by SQuire Rushnell and Louise DuArt.

# Coming Soon!

## Learning and Growing with Laughter Salad
A Mix of Nourishing Activities for Children
Celebrating Nature, Mindfulness, and Stories

THIRD in the *Laughter Salad* Series

Learning and Growing with Laughter Salad

Teachers and counselors will love the stories and activities for children in this sincere, yet playful, book. Kimberly tells what she learned from children around the world and the nourishing activities she created that celebrate nature, mindfulness, and personal stories. This *Laughter Salad* book helps all of us find simple ways to connect with our hearts, the world around us, and our dreams. Help yourself to a serving of *Learning and Growing with Laughter Salad* for nourishment of your mind, body, and spirit. Coming soon!

# List of Illustrations

1. *Laughter Salad for Little Ones* image, front and back cover design, Kimberly Ann Borin, ©2013
2. Laughter Salad for Little Ones — Affirmation for A, Kimberly Ann Borin, ©2013
3. Laughter Salad for Little Ones — Affirmation for B, Kimberly Ann Borin, ©2013
4. Laughter Salad for Little Ones — Affirmation for C, Kimberly Ann Borin, ©2013
5. Laughter Salad for Little Ones — Affirmation for D, Kimberly Ann Borin, ©2013
6. Laughter Salad for Little Ones — Affirmation for E, Kimberly Ann Borin, ©2013
7. Laughter Salad for Little Ones — Affirmation for F, Kimberly Ann Borin, ©2013
8. Laughter Salad for Little Ones — Affirmation for G, Kimberly Ann Borin, ©2013
9. Laughter Salad for Little Ones — Affirmation for H, Kimberly Ann Borin, ©2013
10. Laughter Salad for Little Ones — Affirmation for I, Kimberly Ann Borin, ©2013
11. Laughter Salad for Little Ones — Affirmation for J, Kimberly Ann Borin, ©2013
12. Laughter Salad for Little Ones — Affirmation for K, Kimberly Ann Borin, ©2013
13. Laughter Salad for Little Ones — Affirmation for L, Kimberly Ann Borin, ©2013
14. Laughter Salad for Little Ones — Affirmation for M, Kimberly Ann Borin, ©2013
15. Laughter Salad for Little Ones — Affirmation for N, Kimberly Ann Borin, ©2013
16. Laughter Salad for Little Ones — Affirmation for O, Kimberly Ann Borin, ©2013

17. Laughter Salad for Little Ones — Affirmation for P, Kimberly Ann Borin, ©2013
18. Laughter Salad for Little Ones — Affirmation for Q, Kimberly Ann Borin, ©2013
19. Laughter Salad for Little Ones — Affirmation for R, Kimberly Ann Borin, ©2013
20. Laughter Salad for Little Ones — Affirmation for S, Kimberly Ann Borin, ©2013
21. Laughter Salad for Little Ones — Affirmation for T, Kimberly Ann Borin, ©2013
22. Laughter Salad for Little Ones — Affirmation for U, Kimberly Ann Borin, ©2013
23. Laughter Salad for Little Ones — Affirmation for V, Kimberly Ann Borin, ©2013
24. Laughter Salad for Little Ones — Affirmation for W, Kimberly Ann Borin, ©2013
25. Laughter Salad for Little Ones — Affirmation for X, Kimberly Ann Borin, ©2013
26. Laughter Salad for Little Ones — Affirmation for Y, Kimberly Ann Borin, ©2013
27. Laughter Salad for Little Ones — Affirmation for Z, Kimberly Ann Borin, ©2013
28. Laughter Salad for Little Ones – Peace Page 1, Kimberly Ann Borin, ©2013
29. Laughter Salad for Little Ones – Peace Page 2, Kimberly Ann Borin, ©2013
30. Laughter Salad for Little Ones – Peace Page 3, Kimberly Ann Borin, ©2013
31. Laughter Salad for Little Ones – Peace Page 4, Kimberly Ann Borin, ©2013

Made in the USA
Charleston, SC
23 November 2016